BRAIN ACADEMY

Steph King
and
Richard Cooper

MATHS CHALLENGES

TEACHER'S BOOK 2
For more able mathematicians in Year 3

Rising Stars UK Ltd, 7 Hatchers Mews, Bermondsey Street, London SE1 3GS

www.risingstars-uk.com

Published in association with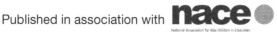

Every effort has been made to trace copyright holders and obtain their permission for the use of copyright materials. The authors and publisher will gladly receive information enabling them to rectify any error or omission in subsequent editions.

The right of Steph King and Richard Cooper to be identified as the authors of this work has been asserted by them in accordance with the Copyright, Design and Patents Act 1998.

Published 2014
Reprinted 2015
Text, design and layout © Rising Stars UK Ltd. 2014

Authors: Steph King and Richard Cooper
Series Consultant: Cherri Moseley
Text design and typesetting: Mark Walker
Cover design: Lon Chan, Words & Pictures Ltd, London
Publisher: Fiona Lazenby
Editorial: Lynette Woodward and Tom Fryer, Sparks Publishing Services, Ltd
Illustrations: Bill Greenhead (characters), Mark Walker and Steve Evans

All rights reserved. No part of this publication may be reproduced, stored in a retrieval system, or transmitted, in any form by any means, electronic, mechanical, photocopying, recording or otherwise, without the prior permission of Rising Stars.

British Library Cataloguing in Publication Data.
A CIP record for this book is available from the British Library.

ISBN: 978-1-78339-235-3

Printed by: Ashford Colour Press Ltd

Pages 6–7, TASC: Thinking Actively in a Social Context © Belle Wallace 2004

Contents

Introduction		4
Mission 2.1:	That Sinking Feeling...	10
Mission 2.2:	Don't Get Blown Away	12
Mission 2.3:	Tomb Savers!	14
Mission 2.4:	Gammon Goes Ape	16
Mission 2.5:	Lions on the Loose!	18
Mission 2.6:	The 'Playground Games'	20
Mission 2.7:	The 'Shardome'	22
Mission 2.8:	Balloon Race	24
Mission 2.9:	Bathing for Birdies!	26
Mission 2.10:	Make Way for Segway!	28
Mission 2.11:	Out of This World!	30
Mission 2.12:	Running Robots!	32
Mission 2.13:	Flowers in Space?!	34
Mission 2.14:	Dog Sled Delight!	36
Mission 2.15:	'Old Cogs' to the Rescue!	38
Mission 2.16:	Da Vinci's Downtime	40
Mission 2.17:	Playing the Game!	42
Mission 2.18:	Beetle Mania!	44
Curriculum Mapping Grid		46

Introduction

WELCOME TO THE BRAIN ACADEMY

This series of resources has been developed specifically for the 2014 National Curriculum to support the core aims of ensuring children can reason mathematically and solve problems. The materials are ideal for use with more able children who grasp concepts rapidly to provide extra challenge. The All New Brain Academy missions offer rich and sophisticated problems based around content from the current year's Programme of Study before accelerating into new content from the next year. They draw on mathematics content from across the breadth of the Programme of Study and require children to demonstrate their depth of understanding through a range of increasingly sophisticated challenges that require high-level thinking and perseverance.

HOW TO USE THE PUPIL RESOURCES

Within each Mission File there are 18 missions, each of which requires application of mathematics from different areas of the curriculum, so problems are not restricted to one topic. For example, a Mission File may include elements of number, geometry, measurement and statistics and require children to make connections between these areas of mathematics.

The problems can be set so children work on their own, in pairs or in small groups in the mathematics classroom. Working with others will support some of the language demands of the contexts and questions, as well as encouraging collaboration and the use of mathematical vocabulary. The resources also work well for homework or as the focus of a club.

Children should be encouraged to discuss the problems with others and consider different strategies that could be used that provide either a specific or a generic application. For example, making a list is a generic example that will help to develop a systematic approach.

The use of practical resources should be promoted as these can support children in making sense of more complex contexts and provide a visual representation of the problem. Calculators are a useful tool to help children investigate more extensively, especially with more complicated calculations, where the problem solving itself would be impeded by the time required to complete written procedures.

As teachers, we need to model how to take risks and how to be a problem solver. You may find that participating as a problem solver in the group encourages the children to communicate their ideas more effectively and adopt some of the strategies that you apply.

Information will be presented in a variety of forms including tables, charts, graphs, timetables, scales, clocks, geometrical diagrams, and so on.

The introduction to each Mission sets the scene for the problems that the children will need to solve.

The Main Mission (MM) presents more sophisticated problems which may draw on logic, visual problems, patterns and rules, etc. Again, children are required to interpret information represented in different ways.

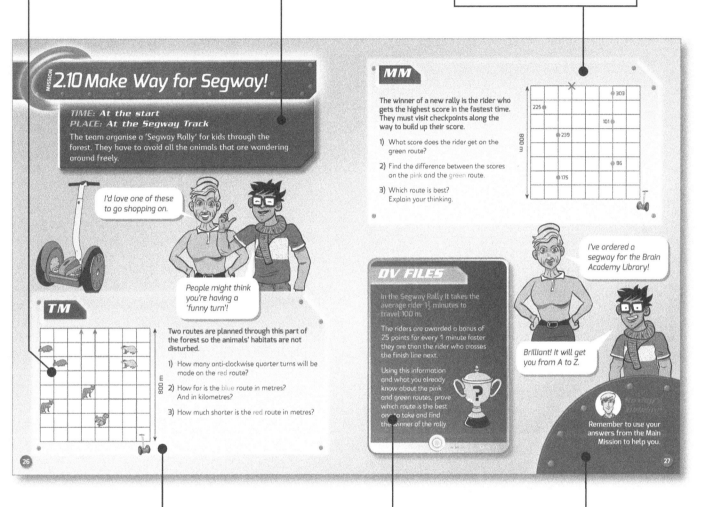

The Training Mission (TM) requires children to use the information given and apply their mathematical knowledge and skills. They will need to reason and explain, thus demonstrating their mathematical fluency.

The Da Vinci Files (DV Files) raise the challenge further and provide a set of more non-routine problems with a greater degree of sophistication. These work well as group tasks to continue to develop reasoning and problem-solving strategies.

Huxley's Helpline reminds the children of vital information or provides hints for how an answer should be presented, for example round all measurements to the nearest whole centimetre. Suggestions are also made to support the process of problem solving, for example record your solutions in a table to help you identify patterns.

PROBLEM-SOLVING STRATEGIES

At the back of each of the Mission Files, children will find some further support in the form of Mission Strategies. These are designed to scaffold the problem-solving process to develop skills generally, in addition to providing specific hints and ideas as starting points for each mission if children find it difficult to make progress.

The TASC Problem Solving Wheel (TASC: Thinking Actively in a Social Context ©Belle Wallace 2004) provides a set of strategies to encourage children to think actively by gathering information, identifying the problem and making a number of decisions about methods and effective ways to communicate ideas. These strategies form valuable discussion points for the teacher and children as some aspects are likely to require further development than others. These are likely to be different for each individual.

Teachers and other adults will find it useful to model some of these processes so that children are clear about each step and, over time, learn to be expert thinkers! In particular, you may find that your more able pupils need to further develop strategies to evaluate, communicate and reflect on their thinking. They should always be encouraged to look for more than one solution and different ways to solve problems.

In addition to the Huxley's Helpline clue within each mission, the children will find a further set of strategies to support each of the challenges. These Mission Strategies may refer to the Training Mission (TM), the Main Mission (MM) or the Da Vinci Files (DV FILES).

The strategies have a range of different purposes. For example, they may be:

- A reminder about valuable pieces of information that may need to be referred to in more than one mission. This is to prompt children to think about what they already know.

- A reference to a conversion that they will need to apply or to the properties of 2-D and 3-D shapes. This is to remind children to draw upon their mathematical knowledge and skills.

- A suggestion of a starting point or a systematic approach. This provides some generic ideas that can be used to solve other problems.

- A recommendation of a way to record or present ideas so that patterns can be identified and any missing solutions found. This provides children with a model to organise their ideas and communicate their thinking.

Children should be encouraged to have a go at the problem first, before referring to the Mission Strategies for help. This will provide a clear picture of what children can do and what skills they can apply independently.

TASC WHEEL

TASC stands for Thinking Actively in a Social Context. Developed by Belle Wallace, Past President of NACE, TASC is a well-researched universal thinking skills framework which empowers learners to:

- work independently yet within an inclusive school policy
- develop skills of research, investigation and problem-solving that can be used across the curriculum
- develop a positive sense of self as an active learner
- develop their abilities using the full range of multiple intelligences
- develop skills of self-assessment.

TASC provides teachers with a framework for:

- lesson planning that systematically develops pupils' thinking and personalises their learning
- effective planning for differentiation and extension
- a holistic approach to incorporating the full range of human abilities
- assessing the processes of pupils' learning.

The TASC Wheel represents a series of thinking skills that an expert thinker uses. An expert has automatised these processes and uses them flexibly, flipping forwards and backwards as the task demands. Very often, teachers are using these processes in their planning and delivery, but they do not usually share their thinking processes with the pupils.

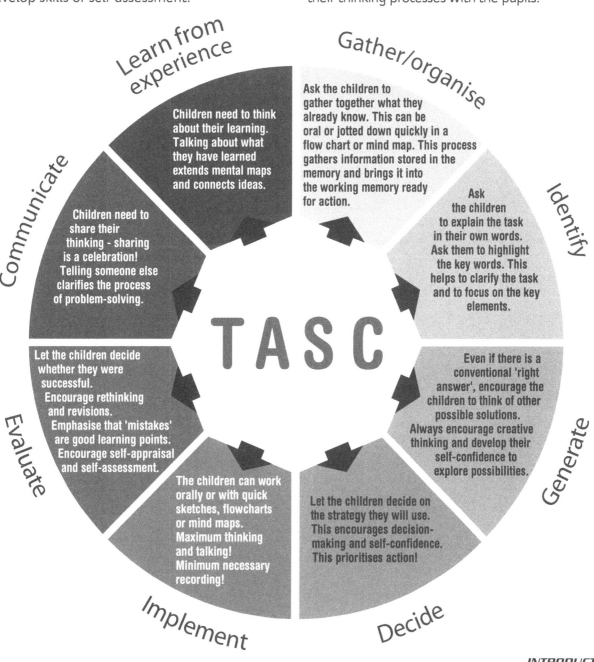

HOW TO USE THE TEACHING RESOURCES

The *All New Brain Academy* Teacher's Books provide the background information needed to summarise each of the problems in the corresponding Mission File, along with a full set of answers and worked examples. The mathematical content for each mission is clearly identified and draws from all areas of the National Curriculum.

All New Brain Academy provides valuable opportunities to assess the depth of children's understanding and the range of strategies they use. For each mission you will find examples of strategies to look out for and any misconceptions that may arise. There may also be suggestions that could be made to help children access the tasks if they are finding it difficult to identify a starting point or keep track of the information or results.

All the challenges draw upon different types of problem solving. These are:

- Finding all possibilities
- Logic problems
- Finding rules and describing patterns
- Diagram problems and visual puzzles
- Word problems (one-, two- or multi-step)

Examples of the first four types in the list above are as follows:

Finding all possibilities	Logic problems
• Finding different possible amounts • Finding different ways to get to an amount • Combinations • Permutations • Finding missing numbers	• Magic squares • Connected clues • Sudoku • Meeting more than one criterion
Finding rules and describing patterns	**Diagram problems and visual puzzles**
• Sequences • Graphs • Determining values that meet a rule	• Identifying shapes hidden in a diagram • Identifying missing angles or lengths of sides • Mazes

These problem-solving types or examples are not listed under the mathematical content in each mission as the majority of the challenges involve a combination of all types of problem-solving. There are also no direct references to reasoning as, like problem solving, this is integral to all missions.

> The Mathematical Content refers to broad themes within the curriculum. Each mission draws on a range of areas and is not focused on one particular objective or topic.

> Each problem is summarised and provides a useful insight into possible strategies, assessment opportunities, ways to support the children, and so on. Sometimes a useful model is also provided.

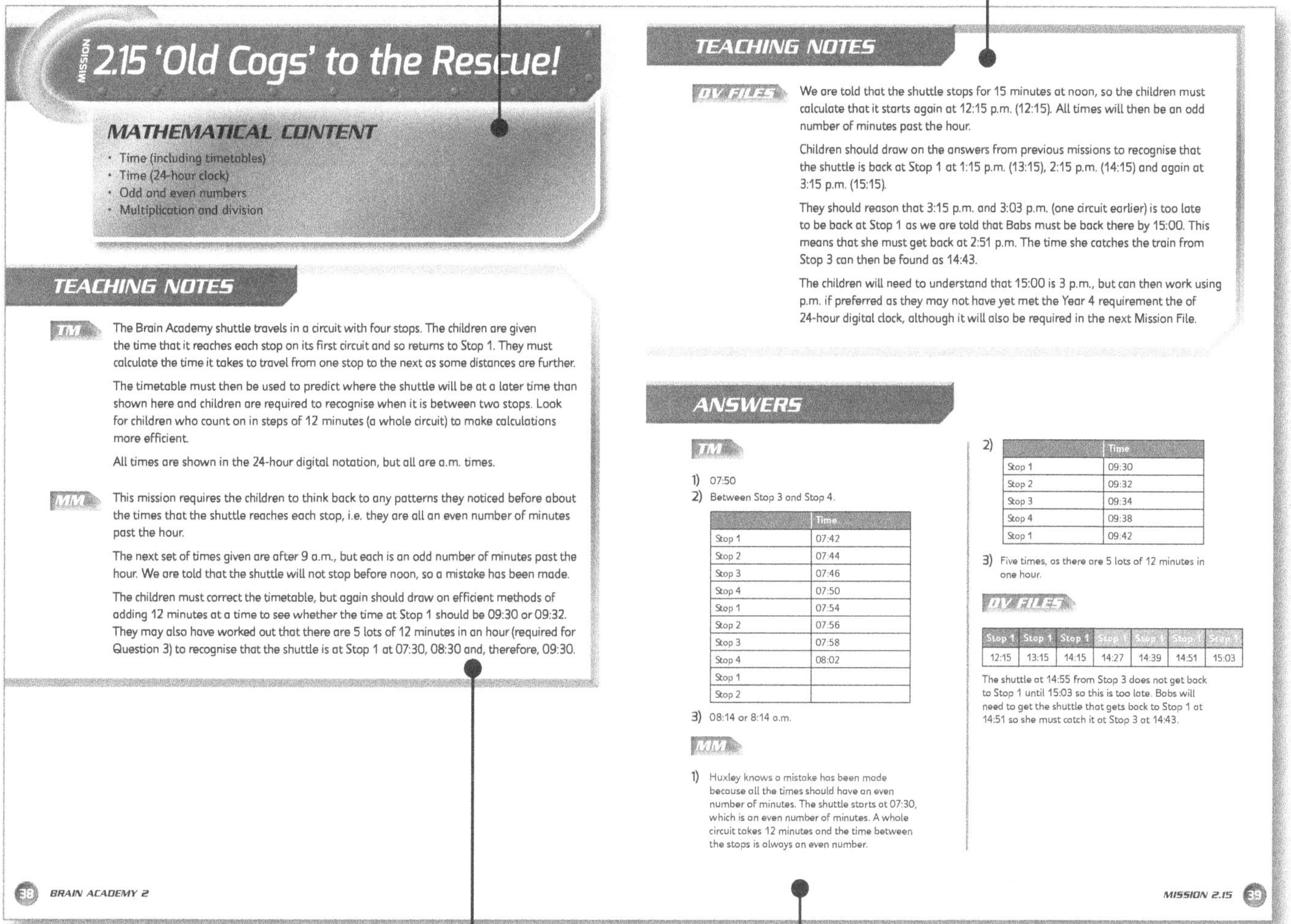

MISSION 2.15 'Old Cogs' to the Rescue!

MATHEMATICAL CONTENT

- Time (including timetables)
- Time (24-hour clock)
- Odd and even numbers
- Multiplication and division

TEACHING NOTES

TM

The Brain Academy shuttle travels in a circuit with four stops. The children are given the time that it reaches each stop on its first circuit and so returns to Stop 1. They must calculate the time it takes to travel from one stop to the next as some distances are further.

The timetable must then be used to predict where the shuttle will be at a later time than shown here and children are required to recognise when it is between two stops. Look for children who count on in steps of 12 minutes (a whole circuit) to make calculations more efficient.

All times are shown in the 24-hour digital notation, but all are a.m. times.

MM

This mission requires the children to think back to any patterns they noticed before about the times that the shuttle reaches each stop, i.e. they are all an even number of minutes past the hour.

The next set of times given are after 9 a.m., but each is an odd number of minutes past the hour. We are told that the shuttle will not stop before noon, so a mistake has been made.

The children must correct the timetable, but again should draw on efficient methods of adding 12 minutes at a time to see whether the time at Stop 1 should be 09:30 or 09:32. They may also have worked out that there are 5 lots of 12 minutes in an hour (required for Question 3) to recognise that the shuttle is at Stop 1 at 07:30, 08:30 and, therefore, 09:30.

TEACHING NOTES

DV FILES

We are told that the shuttle stops for 15 minutes at noon, so the children must calculate that it starts again at 12:15 p.m. (12:15). All times will then be an odd number of minutes past the hour.

Children should draw on the answers from previous missions to recognise that the shuttle is back at Stop 1 at 1:15 p.m. (13:15), 2:15 p.m. (14:15) and again at 3:15 p.m. (15:15).

They should reason that 3:15 p.m. and 3:03 p.m. (one circuit earlier) is too late to be back at Stop 1 as we are told that Babs must be back there by 15:00. This means that she must get back at 2:51 p.m. The time she catches the train from Stop 3 can then be found as 14:43.

The children will need to understand that 15:00 is 3 p.m., but can then work using p.m. if preferred as they may not have yet met the Year 4 requirement the of 24-hour digital clock, although it will also be required in the next Mission File.

ANSWERS

TM

1) 07:50
2) Between Stop 3 and Stop 4.

	Time
Stop 1	07:42
Stop 2	07:44
Stop 3	07:46
Stop 4	07:50
Stop 1	07:54
Stop 2	07:56
Stop 3	07:58
Stop 4	08:02
Stop 1	
Stop 2	

3) 08:14 or 8:14 a.m.

MM

1) Huxley knows a mistake has been made because all the times should have an even number of minutes. The shuttle starts at 07:30, which is an even number of minutes. A whole circuit takes 12 minutes and the time between the stops is always an even number.

2)
	Time
Stop 1	09:30
Stop 2	09:32
Stop 3	09:34
Stop 4	09:38
Stop 1	09:42

3) Five times, as there are 5 lots of 12 minutes in one hour.

DV FILES

Stop 1	Stop 1	Stop 1	Stop 1	Stop 1	Stop 1	Stop 1
12:15	13:15	14:15	14:27	14:39	14:51	15:03

The shuttle at 14:55 from Stop 3 does not get back to Stop 1 until 15:03 so this is too late. Babs will need to get the shuttle that gets back to Stop 1 at 14:51 so she must catch it at Stop 3 at 14:43.

> The notes may also provide a way into the problem and identify the key piece of information that should be used or is pivotal to finding a solution.

> All missions come with a full set of solutions. More complicated questions or problems are accompanied by worked examples and further explanations or guidance.

MISSION 2.1 That Sinking Feeling...

MATHEMATICAL CONTENT

- Place value
- Addition and subtraction (including difference)
- Fractions (including equivalence)
- Counting in fraction steps
- Roman numerals
- Multiplication and division

TEACHING NOTES

TM The Training Mission requires security of place value with thousands and extends to ten thousand.

Children should draw on knowledge of number bonds to count from 6711 to 7000. A column method would be inappropriate here as the numbers are close in proximity and the larger number is a multiple of 1000.

The difference between 6711 and 10911 must then be found. Look for children who recognise or can explain that the answer will be a multiple of 100 as both numbers end in 11.

A range of methods may be used here, including the column method, but a counting on method to find the difference should be explored, e.g. count on 4000 to reach 10,711 and then add a further 200.

MM A problem with the power in the submarine introduces fractions and counting in tenths. The scale extends from zero to three as children are expected to work with fractions beyond one.

However, they must first recognise the equivalence of $2\frac{1}{2}$ and $2\frac{5}{10}$ to help make sense of the diagram.

The questions require the children to reason about a mistake made my Hailey and explain what she has done wrong. Counting in fractions is essential if children are to make sense of adding and subtracting them.

The danger zone is shown as $\frac{7}{10}$. The power will drop 11 steps of $\frac{1}{10}$ or $1\frac{1}{10}$ to enter this zone.

TEACHING NOTES

DV FILES

The clues for each of the single digits used in the code are shown as a calculation using Roman numerals. Clues include the effect of multiplying by one and also subtracting 10. Look for children who still apply knowledge about our number system when making sense of these calculations.

Once all five digits are found, the children must investigate different permutations to find all possible codes.

As two digits are the same, and we know that they must be the first and last digit in the code, there will be far fewer possibilities than codes with five different digits that can be in any position.

Look for children using systematic methods to ensure that no codes are missed. You may need to suggest ways of keeping a digit constant.

ANSWERS

TM

1) 289 m
2) 4200 m

MM

1) $1\frac{8}{10}$
2) If it had dropped $\frac{8}{10}$ it would be pointing to $1\frac{7}{10}$. It has dropped $\frac{7}{10}$.
3) $1\frac{1}{10}$.

DV FILES

4	3	9	1	4
4	3	1	9	4
4	9	3	1	4
4	9	1	3	4
4	1	9	3	4
4	1	3	9	4

MISSION 2.1

MISSION 2.2 Don't Get Blown Away

MATHEMATICAL CONTENT

- Turns (clockwise and anti-clockwise)
- Fraction of a full turn
- Time (hours, days and months)
- Subtraction
- Direction (eight point compass)
- Equivalence
- Distance (km)
- Multiplication and division

TEACHING NOTES

TM The children are provided with some facts about hurricanes. They should use this information, and knowledge of the world, to find out the direction in which the hurricane rotates around the 'eye' of the storm in Australia and Canada. These are described as clockwise and anti-clockwise.

Children are required to apply knowledge of the number of days in each month to calculate and compare the lengths of the hurricane seasons in the Atlantic and in the Eastern Pacific.

Look for children using efficient strategies to find the total number of days in the Atlantic. Do they use addition or recognise that they can start with 30 × 5 and then add the extra 3 days?

To find the difference, children should notice that both seasons end on the same date, so rather than calculating the length of the whole season in the East Pacific, they can simply find the number of days from 15th May until the last day of May, as the Atlantic season starts on 1st June.

MM The Main Mission focuses on direction using the eight point compass. However, the children will also need to apply knowledge of fractions of a turn to describe how the direction changes.

A map is then used to show some of the nearby towns that could be affected by the hurricane. However, North is not shown in the same direction as the compass, and children must reason as to why Mason mistakenly thinks that the hurricane is heading to Shady Shallows.

TEACHING NOTES

DV FILES

This problem explores the minimum and maximum distance a hurricane can travel every hour based on given information. The children should apply methods of multiplication using partitioning and doubling, along with addition and halving, etc. to find the minimum and maximum distances after a certain number of hours. Some children may even use a short method of multiplication, but this is unnecessary for the majority of the calculations.

We already know that the hurricane is heading towards Poppy Springs, which is 72 km away. It is currently 10:30 a.m., so the children need to calculate the earliest and latest time it could arrive. They should use methods of partitioning or other known facts to identify that the additional 8 km (72 km = 64 km + 8 km) requires them to find the different fractions of an hour needed.

ANSWERS

TM

1) Canada — anti-clockwise
   Australia — clockwise

2) 1st June to 30th November.

June	July	August	September	October	November
30	31	31	30	31	30

The Atlantic season is 183 days, which can be calculated as 30 × 5 days + 3 days.

3) 17 days longer.

MM

1) Northwest (NW).
2) Half turn clockwise or anti-clockwise.
   Two quarter turns clockwise or anti-clockwise.
   Two right angle turns clockwise or anti-clockwise.
3) Mason has made a mistake because Shady Shallows is in a NE direction, but Poppy Springs is NW. He has not realised that the map has been drawn with North facing a different way.

DV FILES

1)

	In 3 hours	In 6 hours	In 7½ hours	In 10 hours	In 20 hours
16 km each hour	48 km	96 km	120 km	160 km	320 km
32 km each hour	96 km	192 km	240 km	320 km	640 km

2) 72 km = 32 km + 32 km + 8 km or
   72 km = 16 km + 16 km + 16 km + 16 km + 8 km.
   Earliest time is in $2\frac{1}{4}$ hours so 12:45 p.m. and latest is in $4\frac{1}{2}$ hours so 3 p.m.

MISSION 2.2

MISSION 2.3 Tomb Savers!

MATHEMATICAL CONTENT

- Length (m and cm)
- Properties of 2-D shapes
- Perimeter
- Addition and subtraction
- Multiplication and division
- Statistics (pictograms)
- Counting in multiples of 4 and 6
- Mass (g and kg)
- Place value
- Equivalence

TEACHING NOTES

TM The first question in this mission requires several steps in order to prove that Mason does indeed have some string remaining. Children must draw on knowledge of properties of 2-D shapes to recognise that the equilateral triangle has sides of equal length and that this is also the case for the regular octagon.

Measurements are given in centimetres only or in mixed units of metres and centimetres so will need to be converted to the same unit before calculating. The rectangle has sides of 86 cm and 1 m 24 cm; the equilateral triangle has sides of 99 cm; the regular octagon has sides of 60 cm.

Look for the different methods of addition or multiplication (including doubling) that children use to find the different perimeters, e.g. do they use the related fact 6 × 8 to help calculate 60 × 8 or calculate 99 × 3 as 100 × 3 and then adjust?

MM In the Main Mission, the number of different pieces of treasure found in Area A are shown as a pictogram. The scale is not given, and the children need to use the clue about the number of lamps found in Area B to find the number found at Area A. From here, they can identify the scale.

In addition to comparing the number of treasures using the pictogram, they must also decide how a pictogram with a scale of 6 will show a total of 27 jewels. They should immediately recognise that 27 is not in a count of 6 starting from zero and so a fraction ($\frac{1}{2}$ in this case) of the symbol will need to be used.

TEACHING NOTES

DV FILES

This is a finding all possibilities problem. The children are given the total mass on the scales in kilograms and the weight of each sculpture and lamp in grams so they will need to convert 4 kg to 4000 g as a starting point. They should investigate to find how many pieces of each treasure could on be on the scales.

There are six possible solutions here and children should be encouraged to find all of them.

Look for those who draw on multiplication facts (e.g. 4 × 10 and 8 × 5) and place value to help make decisions.

You may want to suggest that a table is used to keep track of solutions and to organise thinking.

ANSWERS

TM

1) Area 1 needs 4 m 20 cm.
   Area 2 needs 297 cm or 2 m 97 cm.
   Area 3 needs 480 cm or 4 m 80 cm.
   Total string required is 11 m 97 cm.
2) 3 cm left over.

MM

1) 4
2) 14 jewels and 10 precious stone sculptures, so 4 more jewels.
3)

jewels

DV FILES

Gold lamps 800g	Precious stone sculptures 400 g	Total
5	0	800 g × 5 = 4000 g
0	10	400 g × 10 = 4000 g
4	2	800 g × 4 = 3200 g 400 g × 2 = 800 g
3	4	800 g × 3 = 2400 g 400 g × 4 = 1600 g
2	6	800 g × 2 = 1600 g 400 g × 6 = 2400 g
1	8	800 g × 1 = 800 g 400 g × 8 = 3200 g

MISSION 2.3

MISSION 2.4 Gammon Goes Ape

MATHEMATICAL CONTENT

- Place value
- Reading and writing numbers
- 2-D shapes
- Number order and position (including half way etc.)
- Subtraction (difference)
- Time (analogue and digital)

TEACHING NOTES

TM The children are presented with five numbered art pieces that should be listed in Gammon's book.

They should be placed in order and each should also be written in words. All numbers contain common digits 0, 3, 4 or 7 so that children must really think about place value.

The art pieces are 2-D shapes so each should be named. Look out for and correct children using the term 'diamond' rather than the mathematical name 'rhombus.'

One piece, 3708, has already been entered into the book, but a place value error has been made when writing the number in words. The children must also identify and sketch a possible shape of the piece from the description given.

MM The team suddenly realise that some of the art pieces are missing and are not where they are supposed to be.

The children need to identify the number of the missing pieces using the clues given. They must draw upon knowledge of finding the difference to help find the half-way point and the third-of-the-way point.

A common error here is to miss out the final step of the calculation that is needed when the smallest number is not zero, i.e. adding 60 onto 735 for the square. This is predominantly due to the final step not being necessary when finding the half-way point between, say 0 and 800, as adding 0 has no effect. Children learn about adding and subtracting zero in Year 1.

TEACHING NOTES

DV FILES

To introduce this mission, two times are displayed. One is shown on an analogue clock (time of last full check) and the other on a digital one (time pieces reported as missing). Security guards patrol every quarter of an hour.

Children should find the time of each of these patrols and reason about when the pieces must have gone missing.

They should use what they know about the number of quarters of an hour there are in one hour to work through the problem efficiently. Look for children who reason that the last full check was 1:50 p.m. so we immediately know that there was one at 2:50 p.m. (an hour later) but not one at 3:50 p.m. as the paintings had already gone. All other patrols can easily be listed, with the first being 2:05 p.m.

ANSWERS

TM

1)

Number	Number in words	Shape name
0407	Four hundred and seven	parallelogram
0437	Four hundred and thirty-seven	pentagon
0473	Four hundred and seventy-three	trapezium
4037	Four thousand and thirty-seven	octagon
4073	Four thousand and seventy-three	rhombus

2)

3708	Three thousand, seven hundred and eight	Triangle with 3 acute angles

Eg.

MM

1) Square is 0795.
   Either   855 − 735 = 120
            120 ÷ 2 = 60, so square is 735 + 60.
   or   855 + 735 = 1590
            1590 ÷ 2 = 795.

   Triangle is 0775.
   Use what we know about the difference between 855 and 735.
   120 ÷ 3 = 40, so triangle is 735 + 40.

2) 20

DV FILES

The last full check was at 1:50 p.m. so the security guards patrolled at 2:05 p.m., 2:20 p.m., 2:35 p.m., 2:50 p.m., 3:05 p.m., 3:20 p.m. and 3:35 p.m.

The paintings must have been stolen between 3:35 p.m. and 3:43 p.m.

MISSION 2.4

MISSION 2.5 Lions on the Loose!

MATHEMATICAL CONTENT

- Recognising and calculating fractions of amounts
- Mass (kg)
- Sequences
- Place values
- Addition and subtraction
- Multiplication (doubling)

TEACHING NOTES

TM The task requires the children to reason about the clues given and try out various combinations and permutations to find a set of solutions.

It may be useful to present one clue at a time so that children can think about one variable in the problem before moving on to another. Decisions can then be amended if possibilities no longer suit each subsequent clue.

Children could use cubes or counters to represent the cubs, and a grid to represent the seven classrooms. Counters can be moved and rearranged to help find the different possible locations of all six cubs.

MM In this mission the children will need to refer back to their solutions from the Training Mission to help make decisions about possible fractions of 18 kg.

Children must first recognise that 18 kg is the whole and then identify the different fractions that one cub, two cubs or three cubs represent, i.e. $\frac{1}{6}$, $\frac{1}{3}$ and $\frac{1}{2}$.

Fraction bars or other visuals may support the children when calculating, e.g.

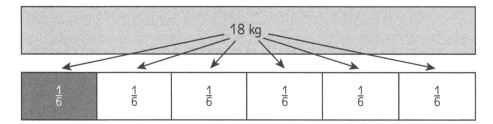

In Question 3 they must find a way to explain why 12 kg was not used in any of the classrooms. They should recognise 12 kg as more than $\frac{1}{2}$ of 18 kg and, using what they know from Question 1, explain that largest mass used is 9 kg.

Look for children who can also show that 12 kg is $\frac{2}{3}$ of 18 kg.

TEACHING NOTES

DV FILES

The cubs can move in a horizontal, vertical or diagonal direction. They must each step on at least three squares in the grid.

Children should be encouraged to work on one cub at a time and to look at the problem as a whole to find a starting point. This may not always be the first clue or example. In this problem, the middle cub follows the easiest sequence to reach the food whilst the top cub follows the most challenging one.

The level of challenge is also raised by the inclusion of question marks that represent missing values in two of the sequences.

Calculators can be used to check possible solutions and further extend the problem by exploring the inverse, i.e. confirming a correct solution for the bottom cub by adding 600 to 2040 and then to 3240 to return to the start number 2640.

ANSWERS

TM

Class 1	Class 2	Class 3	Class 4	Class 5	Class 6	Class 7
	3 cubs		1 cub		2 cubs	
3 cubs			1 cub		2 cubs	
3 cubs			1 cub			2 cubs
	3 cubs		1 cub			2 cubs
	2 cubs		1 cub		3 cubs	
2 cubs			1 cub		3 cubs	
2 cubs			1 cub			3 cubs
	2 cubs		1 cub			3 cubs

MM

1) 1 cub = $\frac{1}{6}$, 2 cubs = $\frac{1}{3}$ and 3 cubs = $\frac{1}{2}$.
2) 3 kg.
3) 12 kg is $\frac{2}{3}$ of the total mass of food. We know that the largest fraction used was $\frac{1}{2}$ or that $\frac{2}{3}$ of 6 cubs is 4 cubs and we know that there were not 4 cubs in any classroom.
4) 2 cubs will have 6 kg and 3 cubs will have 9 kg.

DV FILES

35		29	19
70	90	49	
140	280	79	?
	?	1020	169
3240	2640	2040	Food

Door

Top cub
35, 70, 140, 280, 560, 1020, 2040
Rule — double the number each time.

Middle cub
19, 29, 49, 79, 119, 169
Rule — add an extra 10 each time.

Bottom cub
3240, 2640, 2040
Rule — subtract 600 each time.

MISSION 2.5

MISSION 2.6 The 'Playground Games'

MATHEMATICAL CONTENT

- Multiples of 8 and 20
- Counting in fractions steps
- Patterns and sequences
- Addition and subtraction
- Multiplication and division

TEACHING NOTES

TM The children must find the missing values on each of the hopscotch games by first finding the rule that governs them.

Look for children who apply knowledge of place value to multiples of 2 to identify the multiples of 20.

In Mason's hopscotch a pattern using multiples of 8 is made, however, the children are required to go beyond the twelfth multiple and as far as a three-digit number.

Huxley's hopscotch follows a sequence of adding $\frac{5}{8}$ each time from a mixed number. This is trickier than working in tenths (as in Mission 2.1) as the children need to remember that they are drawing on bonds of 8, rather than the more familiar bonds of 10 used in our counting system to reach a boundary. Look for children who make use of number line or other resources to support here.

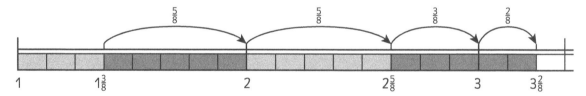

MM This is a logic problem where children need to decide how many different games of conkers can be played.

A table is introduced as a way of working with logic problems of this nature.

The key is to remember that a team member cannot play themselves and that a pair can only play each other once for this to count as a 'different' solution. The children are instructed to complete the shading on the table based on this reasoning. They should find that six different games can be played.

A set of three clues reveals how many games some of the Brain Academy members won or lost. Now, using this, the children must find out who was the winner in each of the six games and complete the table.

TEACHING NOTES

DV FILES

The game of 'It' has been developed here so that children score points when they catch the six players in different zones. All zones have points that are multiples of 5.

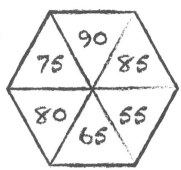

Children are required to explore different possibilities to suit the criteria given in the problem, e.g. to find the highest possible score or the different ways the chaser can score 390 points.

Look for children who recognise that catching all children in zone 90 will score the most points (and in 55 the least) and use knowledge of multiplication facts and place value to calculate. Children may also use known facts, such as 3 × 9 = 27 to find 6 × 9 by doubling 27 along with place value to calculate 90 × 6. These strategies should be encouraged as this makes the connections between the multiplication tables, draws on commutativity and supports with facts that may not yet be known, e.g. multiplication facts of 6 is in the Year 4 Programme of Study.

ANSWERS

TM

1) 1 – all multiples of 20 starting from 20 or add 20 each time.
   2 – all multiples of 8 or add 8 each time starting from 32.
   3 – add $\frac{5}{8}$ each time.

2) 1 – 160 and 180.
   2 – 96 and 104.
   3 – $3\frac{7}{8}$ and $5\frac{6}{8}$.

MM

1)

	Huxley	Babs	Mason	Gammon
Huxley				
Babs				Babs
Mason				
Gammon				

6 games:
Huxley/Babs, Huxley/Mason, Huxley/Gammon, Babs/Mason, Babs/Gammon, Mason/Gammon

2)

	Huxley	Babs	Mason	Gammon
Huxley		Huxley	Huxley	Huxley
Babs			Babs	Babs
Mason				Gammon
Gammon				

DV FILES

1) Highest is 90 × 6 = 540 points.
2) Lowest is 55 × 6 = 330 points.
3) 390 points can be scored with:
   75 × 2 and 55 × 2 and 65 × 2
   90 × 1 and 55 × 4 and 80 × 1
   65 × 6
   75 × 3 and 55 × 3
   75 × 1 and 65 × 4 and 55 × 1
   85 × 1 and 65 × 3 and 55 × 2
   85 × 2 and 55 × 4
   80 × 2 and 65 × 1 and 55 × 3

MISSION 2.7 The 'Shardome'

MATHEMATICAL CONTENT

- Parallel and perpendicular lines
- Angles
- Fractions of shapes (including equivalence)
- Counting in fraction steps
- Height and distance (metres)
- Addition
- Multiplication (including doubling)
- Place value

TEACHING NOTES

TM Two windows on the 'Shardome' are shown, each with a different design. In geometry work, children will have identified and drawn pairs of perpendicular and parallel lines.

In this problem, Window B is likely to be seen as being trickier as many of the pairs of lines are not horizontal or vertical. Children should be encouraged to use strategies such as turning the book or using the corner of a ruler or paper to confirm that the lines meet at a right angle and are, therefore, perpendicular.

The children must also identify any acute angles on Window B. Again, look for any strategies they may use to check, e.g. less than the corner of a ruler or set square.

MM The Main Mission focuses on fractions of a shape, but divided in a way that has not resulted in all equal parts.

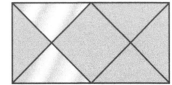

The key to this task is recognising that the square in the middle of the design is equivalent to two of the triangular parts. This means that the fraction shaded is $\frac{2}{8}$ and can be written as $\frac{1}{4}$.

The children are asked to find three alternative ways to show $\frac{1}{4}$ on the window design. Look for those who are less confident to shade two eighths at opposite ends of the window.

The final task involves counting in fraction steps of $\frac{2}{8}$ (or $\frac{1}{4}$) up to $4\frac{3}{4}$. Children should demonstrate fluency by counting each whole as four quarters and simply multiply four wholes by 4 and add the additional three steps of $\frac{1}{4}$.

TEACHING NOTES

DV FILES

The vital piece of information in this problem is remembering that the distance given does not represent a return journey. Children should use methods of doubling, not only initially to find the distance of the return journey, but also double the result of the second trip to find the fourth and the fifth trip to find the tenth.

Look for methods children use to double, e.g. partitioning, doubling and then recombining. Also be aware of those who simply use repeated addition for all trips and do not recognise the task as being one where methods of multiplication will be more efficient, particularly from the fifth trip to the tenth trip.

ANSWERS

TM

1) Window B

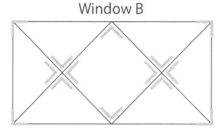

2) Window A has eight pairs of perpendicular lines and Window B has 14.
   Window B has six more pairs.
3) Four pairs.
4) 12.

MM

1) $\frac{1}{4}$ or $\frac{2}{8}$
2) E.g.

3) 19 lots of $\frac{1}{4}$ which can be calculated as 4 × 4 + 3.

DV FILES

After 1st change	After 2nd change	After 3rd change	After 4th change	After 5th change	After 10th change
612 m	1224 m	1836 m	2448 m	3060 m	6120 m

MISSION 2.7

MISSION 2.8 Balloon Race

MATHEMATICAL CONTENT

- 3-D shapes
- Properties of 3-D shapes
- Distance (km)
- Time – analogue clock
- Time – calculating intervals
- Multiplication and division
- Money
- Even numbers

TEACHING NOTES

TM   A set of 3-D shapes must be identified from 2-D drawings of the balloons that are about to cross the channel. The children must then use what they know about the properties to identify the number of rectangular faces and straights edges that are on the balloons.

Children should notice that this cuboid has six rectangular faces and does not have square ends that may be found on other example cuboids. Also, reasoning about the number of 'unseen' faces on the pentagonal prism may be more challenging for some.

A set of solid shapes can be used if needed or for checking, but this should be after the children have had a chance to reason about the properties first as this will be a useful assessment opportunity.

MM We are told that the race started at noon and that the analogue clock shows the time it is now. Children should be familiar with and use vocabulary such as o'clock, a.m./p.m., morning, afternoon, noon and midnight. They must find the time the race has taken so far by calculating the interval.

A number line from 0 to 35 km shows the position of the balloons at the given time. The children will need to draw on multiplication and division facts (or notice that the 35 km journey has been divided into fifths) to help find how far each balloon has travelled so far.

Balloon C requires them to find the mid-point between 21 km and 28 km.

BRAIN ACADEMY 2

TEACHING NOTES

DV FILES

This is a finding all possibilities problem that must suit a given set of criteria, i.e. no one receives less than £15 of the prize money and the team was made up of an even number of people.

Huxley's Helpline encourages the children to use a table to set out their results clearly.

The children must first find a starting point, which may well be to halve £180 to find the amount won by two team members or use place value to divide £180 by 10 to find a possible solution. Look for children who use more appropriate starting points rather than randomly picking an even number to try.

Look for children who use related facts, i.e. 18 ÷ 6 to help find 180 ÷ 6 or use halving and halving again to divide by 4, etc.

ANSWERS

TM

1) cuboid and cone
2) 11
3) 43

MM

1) 3 hours and 35 minutes.
2) Balloon A – 7 km;
   Balloon B – 14 km;
   Balloon C – 24$\frac{1}{2}$ km.

DV FILES

Number in team	2	4	6	8	10	12
Equal share of prize money	£90	£45	£30	£22.50	£18	£15

MISSION 2.8

MISSION 2.9 Bathing for Birdies!

MATHEMATICAL CONTENT

- 2-D shapes
- Multiplication and division
- Capacity (ml)
- Addition and subtraction
- Fractions of 2-D shapes

TEACHING NOTES

TM When lines are drawn from the vertices and meet at a central point of a regular shape a number of equal parts are created. The key to this problem is to recognise that the number of equal sections the shapes will have is equal to its number of sides. Children could go on to check this for equilateral triangles, regular heptagons and regular nonagons, etc. beyond the problem here.

Children should recognise the shapes from the names given and make comparisons. When finding out how many more sections three octagonal baths have than three pentagonal ones, look for children who recognise that one octagonal bath has three more sections, so they simply have to multiply 3 × 3. This is a more efficient way than finding the difference between 5 × 3 and 8 × 3.

MM The relationship between litres and millilitres must be used in this problem so that the calculations needed can be identified.

Children should draw on the related facts 30 ÷ 5 and 30 ÷ 6 and knowledge of place value to calculate 3000 ml ÷ 5 and 3000 ml ÷ 6. An efficient way to calculate 3000 ml ÷ 8 is to use a method of repeated halving or to partition 3000 ml into 2400 ml and 600 ml. They may also use a 'chunking' or more formal written method of short division for this last calculation, but this should be challenged if used for the two previous ones.

The final question is a reminder about the size of unit fractions when the whole is the same, i.e. $\frac{1}{5}$ is greater than $\frac{1}{8}$.

TEACHING NOTES

DV FILES

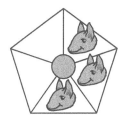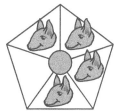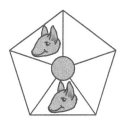

This problem extends the use of fractions beyond one. Having first identified the fraction of sections filled by squirrels in each bird bath, they should then notice that the two squirrels from the third bath ($\frac{2}{5}$) can be put in the first bath ($\frac{3}{5}$) to fill it ($\frac{5}{5}$).

They should then identify that $\frac{1}{5}$ of the second bath is still empty and then that $1\frac{1}{4}$ of the three baths is empty.

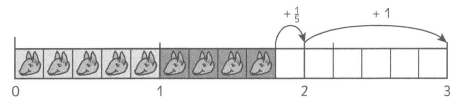

ANSWERS

TM

1) 6

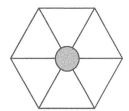

2) The octagonal bath has three more sections than the pentagonal baths so there will be nine more sections in three of these octagonal baths.

3) 12

MM

1) Pentagonal 3000 ml ÷ 5 = 600 ml
2) Hexagonal 3000 ml ÷ 6 = 500 ml
   Octagonal 3000 ml ÷ 8 = 375 ml
3) 225 ml more in the pentagonal because the 3 litres only has to be split into 5 equal parts and not 8. So each of the 5 parts is bigger.

DV FILES

1) $\frac{3}{5}$, $\frac{4}{5}$ and $\frac{2}{5}$
2) $\frac{1}{5}$
3) $1\frac{1}{5}$

MISSION 2.9

MISSION 2.10 Make Way for Segway!

MATHEMATICAL CONTENT

- Turns (quarter turns, clockwise and anti-clockwise)
- Counting in multiples of 100
- Multiplying by 100
- Distance (m and km)
- Addition and subtraction (including difference)
- Time (minutes)

TEACHING NOTES

TM

The problem requires the children to navigate their way around the grid using the red and blue route.

They must consider the number of quarter turns they make in an anti-clockwise direction and calculate distances of each route.

Look for children who rotate the image so that it is easier to identify clockwise and anti-clockwise turns.

Using the measurement given for the length of one side of the grid, children should recognise that the sides of each of the smaller squares are 100 m.

Look for children who count accurately in hundreds across the thousands boundary or recognise that the route follows 14 lengths of 100 m and simply uses place value to scale up to 1400 m. Knowledge of the relationship between metres and kilometres is necessary to convert the distance into 1 km 400 m or even refined to 1.4 km.

MM

Still applying the measurements they established in the Training Mission, the children should explore and compare the length of two routes and the number of points they score on each.

Look for children who use knowledge of number bonds when adding 175 + 239 + 225 and may even apply them if they add 101 and 303 together first and then add 86.

Children are required to reason about the two routes and explain that even though more points are gained on the pink route, the green route is shorter.

TEACHING NOTES

DV FILES

In the final problem the children must find a way to prove which rider is the winner of the race.

They are told that it takes a rider $1\frac{1}{2}$ minutes to ride 100 m so decisions should be made based on the information that they already have from the previous mission, i.e. the pink route is 400 m longer.

The children should recognise that the calculation needed is $1\frac{1}{2}$ minutes × 4, which then proves that the pink route takes 6 minutes longer.

However, the problem is not complete. Riders get bonus points for being faster so the rider on the green route will get extra points to add on to 490.

Look for children who spot that the original difference between scores from the Main Mission was 149 and the green rider has just scored an extra 150 points so now has one point more. This is a more efficient method than adding 490 + 150 and then comparing the total with 639 scored by the pink rider.

ANSWERS

TM

1) 2
2) 1400 m or 1 km 400 m or 1.4 km
3) 300 m shorter

MM

1) 303 + 101 + 86 = 490
2) Pink is 225 + 239 + 175 = 639
   Pink is 149 more points
3) It depends. The pink route gets you more points but the green route is 400 m shorter so will be faster.

DV FILES

The rider on the pink route has 400 m further to go. There are 4 lots of 100 metres so will take 4 lots of $1\frac{1}{2}$ minutes more. This is a total of 6 minutes, so the rider on the green route will get a bonus of 25 × 6 points = 150 points. The green total is now 640 points so is the winner by 1 point.

You can also use what you know about the difference of 149 from Mission 2.1 Question 2 to simply see that the green rider has now got one more point.

MISSION 2.10

MISSION 2.11 Out of This World!

MATHEMATICAL CONTENT

- Distance (km)
- Place value
- Time (seconds and years)
- Mass (grams and kilograms)
- Place value
- Addition and subtraction
- Multiplication (including doubling)
- Direction

TEACHING NOTES

TM The Training Mission focuses on facts about meteoroids, meteors and meteorites.

Children are required to use place value to answer questions about distance and mass, i.e. knowing that 0.84 kg is equivalent to 840 g.

Look for children who use knowledge of doubling and place value to calculate 42 km × 20. It is useful to discuss whether the answer is the same if the doubling is done first or last, i.e. 42 × 2 × 10 or 42 × 10 × 2.

This further develops commutativity of multiplication that was introduced in Year 2.

The final question will depend on the current year, but look for any strategies used to bridge the year 2000, e.g. bonds to 100 to count from 1902 to 2000 and then add, say, 14 to reach 2014 or adding 100 using place value to reach 2002 and then adding 12.

MM The children are given details about the distance of the meteor and the space probe from the Moon.

Both measurements are multiples of 10 km, and 100 km in the case of 2400 km. They must calculate the difference between the two distances to find out which is closer to the Moon.

Look for children using mental strategies and simply add 150 km to 1850 km to reach 2000 km and then add a further 400 km. Using a column method involving decomposition is more likely to result in errors here.

Question 2 requires increasing values by steps of 150 km for the meteor and 200 km for the probe over a period of time. Children need to refer back to the distances each are from the Moon to find out which one will reach it first.

Look for use of place values and multiples of two to support calculations for the probe and those who recognise that double 150 km is 300 km, and use this fact to work more efficiently.

TEACHING NOTES

DV FILES

In preparation for translations in Year 4, children must help NASA by giving instructions to land the probe safely on the meteor. However, the task is not straightforward as the probe must be navigated past space meteoroids, which must be avoided.

The children must use the instructions *left*, *right*, *up* and *down* to move the probe, but are reminded in Huxley's Helpline that they must say how many squares to move each time. This is the same language that will be used for translation.

Two possible solutions must be found. Moving counters on a larger version of the grid may be useful.

ANSWERS

TM

1) 420 km in 10 seconds, so 840 km in 20 seconds.
2) 840 g
3) Answer will depend on the current year. At the time of writing this is 2014, so this meteorite landed 112 years ago.

MM

1) 550 km
2) The probe has 2400 km to travel and the meteor has 1850 km

Probe	200 km	400 km	600 km	800 km	1000 km	1200 km	...	2400 km
Meteor	150 km	300 km	450 km	600 km	750 km	900 km		1800 km

The probe will arrive first as the meteor still has 50 km left to travel.

DV FILES

There are several different routes. Here are two examples.

Example 1:
Left 2, down 3, left 2, down 2

Example 2
Down 2, right 1, down 3, left 1, down 1, left 4, up 1

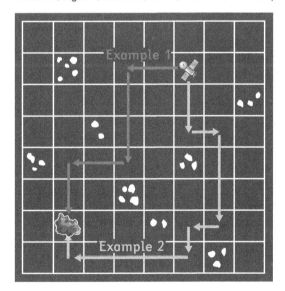

MISSION 2.12 Running Robots!

MATHEMATICAL CONTENT
- Equivalence
- Fractions of amounts (length)
- Length (m and cm)
- Multiplication (including doubling)
- Addition and subtraction

TEACHING NOTES

TM

	Jump 1	Jump 2	Jump 3	Jump 4
ZID	$\frac{7}{10}$ of a metre	$\frac{4}{5}$ of a metre	$1\frac{1}{2}$ metres	
ZAP	50 cm	$\frac{8}{10}$ of a metre	$1\frac{50}{100}$ metres	

The children are given the information above to prove which robot jumps the furthest each time.

They must draw on the knowledge that there are 100 cm in a metre and remember that tenths arise when an object or amount is divided into ten equal parts. This means that $\frac{1}{10}$ m is equivalent to 10 cm.

Once this has been established, all fractions can be shown as centimetres and can be compared.

Mixed numbers are used for Jump 3 and the fraction parts are different in both. Children will need to reason that $\frac{1}{100}$ of a metre is 1 cm as it takes 100 of them to equal the whole, so $\frac{50}{100}$ is 50 cm or that $\frac{50}{100}$ is equivalent to $\frac{1}{2}$.

Children make up their own values for Jump 4 as long as they meet the criteria given. They should recognise $\frac{25}{100}$ as 25 cm and/or the equivalence between $\frac{25}{100}$ and $\frac{1}{4}$.

MM

When a third robot is introduced, Evan is amazed.

The children are required to use the information to find the length of Zeb's jump. These are all written in relation to the jumps in the previous mission, but children will apply methods for doubling and multiplying by 3, 4 and 5.

Look for the strategies children use to multiply. Do they use multiplication facts to help them, e.g. 80 cm × 4 using 8 × 4 × 10, or do they apply a method of repeated addition? Encourage the use of multiplication methods as this will further develop children's multiplicative reasoning skills.

TEACHING NOTES

DV FILES

This is a missing number problem in preparation for work on algebra at the end of Key Stage 2.

Children have been building the foundations of algebra from a very early age, but this problem uses symbols to represent the same numbers in a set of equations so is likely to be more tricky.

Huxley's Helpline makes it clear that each robot retains the same value in all clues.

However, the key here is identifying that the third clue gives us the value of Zap and this can then be used to work out the other values. Children should be encouraged to look at the whole problem first in order to find the most useful starting point.

ANSWERS

TM

1) Jump 1: Zid because $\frac{7}{10}$ of a metre is 70 cm.
   Jump 2: both the same, as $\frac{4}{5}$ m and $\frac{8}{10}$ m are equivalent fractions of a metre.
   Jump 3: both the same, as $1\frac{1}{2}$ m and $1\frac{50}{100}$ m are also equivalent fractions of a metre.

2) E.g. Zid: 2 m 50 cm ($2\frac{1}{2}$ m) and Zap 2 m 25 cm ($2\frac{1}{4}$ m).

MM

	Zeb's jumps
Jump 1	Double Zid's jump	1 m 40 cm
Jump 2	Four times further than Zid's jump	3 m 20 cm
Jump 3	Three times further than Zid's jump	4 m 50 cm
Jump 4	Five times further than Zid's jump	e.g. 12 m 50 cm

DV FILES

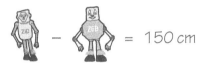 = 150 cm

 = 900 cm

 = 7 metres

ZID	$5\frac{1}{2}$ m
ZAP	$3\frac{1}{2}$ m
ZEB	4 m

MISSION 2.12

MISSION 2.13 Flowers in Space?!

MATHEMATICAL CONTENT
- Arrays
- Multiplication
- Statistics (bar charts)
- Height (cm)
- Addition and subtraction (including difference)

TEACHING NOTES

TM

The total number of plants is displayed as an array. However, within the larger array, smaller ones are used to represent the number of each of the five species planted.

Children should draw on work on arrays to write matching multiplication statements. Look for children who use the commutative law to describe each array in two different ways, e.g. 7 × 4 and 4 × 7.

Also look for children who find it more difficult to describe the array using multiplication and tend to describe it using repeated addition. Further work will need to be done here.

For Question 2, look for children who add up each of the zones instead of simply using the 12 × 10 array.

MM

Although the two bar charts are showing related information, i.e. the height of each plant at the end of week 1 and then week 2, children must check the scales before making any comparisons. The first scale is in intervals of 5 cm, whilst the second is in intervals of 4 cm.

The children are asked to write five different statements to compare the height of the plants at the end of each week. Look for a range of vocabulary used to compare them and challenge the children to use a wider range of words (even suggesting some if necessary), if the statements are all rather similar.

Question 2 requires reasoning about a mistake that Rosa has made. You may find that the children initially think that Rosa is correct, but attention should be drawn to the difference between the values and not that the green bar is the highest on Week 2.

TEACHING NOTES

DV FILES

The Da Vinci mission is all about permutations. Children are encouraged to think about using a code for each of the colours to help their recording.

Look for strategies the children use to keep track of each possibility and recognise any repetitions.

If they have missed several solutions, look together at ways of being systematic, e.g. finding all the possibilities where the yellow plant is first.

They should notice that there are four sets of six possibilities, each set keeping one colour at the front and moving the other three. It may be interesting to ask them to predict what would have happened had there had been only three plants to order, or even five.

ANSWERS

TM

1) Blue   7 × 4 = 28 plants (or 4 × 7)
   Yellow   5 × 2 = 10 plants (or 2 × 5)
   Red   4 × 6 = 24 plants (or 6 × 4)
   Purple   3 × 6 = 18 plants (or 6 × 3)
   Green   5 × 8 = 40 plants (or 8 × 5)

2) 12 × 10 = 120 plants.

MM

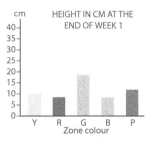
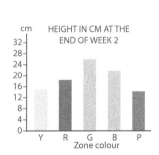

1)

Plant colour	Height at the end of week 1 (cm)	Height at the end of week 1 (cm)	Growth
Yellow	10	15	5
Red	8	18	10
Green	18	26	8
Blue	8	22	14
Purple	12	14	2

E.g. The plant in the yellow zone has grown 5 cm.

The plant in the red zone is now 10 cm taller than it was at the end of week 1.

The plant in the green zone is now 26 cm tall. It has grown 8 cm.

The plant in the blue zone has grown 14 cm more than at the end of week 1.

The purple plant has only grown 2 cm.

2) Rosa thinks this because the green plant is the tallest at the end of Week 2. It is not true because it has only grown 8 cm whereas the plant in the blue zone has grown 14 cm. Although the blue is shorter than the green at the end of Week 2, it has grown the most.

DV FILES

There are 24 possible permutations altogether, e.g. keeping the yellow in the first position there are six possibilities. There are a further six with red always in the first position, another six with green in the first position and a final six with blue in the first position. This makes 24 in total.

MISSION 2.13

MISSION 2.14 Dog Sled Delight!

MATHEMATICAL CONTENT

- Capacity (ml and l)
- Place value
- Rounding
- Multiplication (including doubling) and division
- Money (p and £.p)
- Mass (g and kg)
- Subtraction

TEACHING NOTES

TM The amount of water needed to fill one container is shown on a scale that is labelled in hundreds but in intervals of 20 ml. Children need to draw on facts to identify the size of each interval, e.g. there are five twos in 10 so there are five twenties in 100, or $\frac{1}{5}$ of 100 = 20, or 100 ÷ 5 = 20.

They should then use place value to multiply the amount of water (740 ml) by 10 to find the water needed to fill 10 containers. Look for children who use inappropriate methods, i.e. repeated addition or a more formal method of multiplication.

Finally, they must draw on knowledge that there are 1000 ml in a litre to help round 7400 ml to the nearest litre.

MM Hailey and Gammon must buy enough food for the dogs. The price and weight of two varieties are given so the children can make comparisons. They find the difference between the weights of two tins of each; however, they must use the same unit of measurement. They should use doubling as a strategy here rather than repeated addition or other more formal methods.

The difference can be found in two ways, either by calculating the weight of two tins of each and then finding the difference or by simply finding the difference first between one tin of each, i.e. 1250 g − 825 g = 425 g and then doubling this as there are two of these differences.

Look for the methods children use to find the number of tins that can be bought for £20. Do they use a method of division or scaling up the amounts until they get as close as possible to £20, e.g.

'I know that 10 tins are £8.90 so 20 tins are double this so £17.80. They can still buy some more.'

TEACHING NOTES

DV FILES

The problem asks the children to find out which sled of dogs is cheaper to feed, but it draws on several pieces of key information about the food: weight, price, amount eaten, number of dogs and who likes which food.

The children are required to find the number of tins of each food needed to equal the 10 kg required by each sled. They must remember to round up the number of tins of *Top Dog* to make sure there is enough, whilst the eight *Doggy Delight* tins are exactly 10 kg.

This multistep problem is not yet finished as they find the cost for this meal and then compare.

Look for the different calculation strategies used and fluency in multiplication facts.

You may even want to challenge the children to find out if it is still cheaper to feed Sled 2 after two meals.

In fact, Sled 1 is cheaper as only another 12 tins are needed in addition to the remaining amount from the first meal.

ANSWERS

TM

1) 740 ml
2) 7400 ml
3) 7 litres

MM

1) 2 × 825 grams of *Top Dog* =
   1650g or 1 kg 650g or 1.65 kg

   2 × 1.25 kg of *Doggy Delight* =
   2.5 kg or 2 kg 500 g or 2500 g

   The difference is 2500g – 1650g = 850g

   So 2 tins of *Doggy Delight* are 850 g heavier than 2 tins of *Top Dog*.

2) 22 tins will cost £19.58.
3) 14 tins will cost £19.60.
4) No, because they have only 42p left over from *Top Dog* and 40p left over from *Doggy Delight*. That is 82p in total, but this is not enough for an 89p tin of *Top Dog*.

DV FILES

10 dogs will need 10 kg of food for their first meal.

Sled 1 will need 13 tins of *Top Dog* as 12 tins (9900 g) is not enough.

Sled 2 will need exactly 8 tins of *Doggy Delight*.

Sled 1 will cost 89p × 13 = £ 11.57.

Sled 2 will cost £ 1.40 × 8 = £ 11.20.

It is cheaper to feed the dogs of Sled 2.

MISSION 2.14

MISSION 2.15 'Old Cogs' to the Rescue!

MATHEMATICAL CONTENT
- Time (including timetables)
- Time (24-hour clock)
- Odd and even numbers
- Multiplication and division

TEACHING NOTES

TM The Brain Academy shuttle travels in a circuit with four stops. The children are given the time that it reaches each stop on its first circuit and so returns to Stop 1. They must calculate the time it takes to travel from one stop to the next as some distances are further.

The timetable must then be used to predict where the shuttle will be at a later time than shown here and children are required to recognise when it is between two stops. Look for children who count on in steps of 12 minutes (a whole circuit) to make calculations more efficient.

All times are shown in the 24-hour digital notation, but all are a.m. times.

MM This mission requires the children to think back to any patterns they noticed before about the times that the shuttle reaches each stop, i.e. they are all an even number of minutes past the hour.

The next set of times given are after 9 a.m., but each is an odd number of minutes past the hour. We are told that the shuttle will not stop before noon, so a mistake has been made.

The children must correct the timetable, but again should draw on efficient methods of adding 12 minutes at a time to see whether the time at Stop 1 should be 09:30 or 09:32. They may also have worked out that there are 5 lots of 12 minutes in an hour (required for Question 3) to recognise that the shuttle is at Stop 1 at 07:30, 08:30 and, therefore, 09:30.

TEACHING NOTES

DV FILES

We are told that the shuttle stops for 15 minutes at 12:30 p.m., so the children must calculate that it starts again at 12:45 p.m. All times will then be an odd number of minutes past the hour.

Children should draw on the answers from previous missions to recognise that the shuttle is back at Stop 1 at 1:45 p.m. (13:45), 2:45 p.m. (14:45) and again at 3:45 p.m. (15:45).

They should reason that 3:45 p.m. and 3:33 p.m. (one circuit earlier) is too late to be back at Stop 1 as we are told that Babs must be back there by 15:30. This means that she must get back at 3:21 p.m. The time she catches the train from Stop 3 can then be found as 15:13.

The children will need to understand that 15:00 is 3 p.m., but can then work using p.m. if preferred as they may not have yet met the Year 4 requirement of the 24-hour digital clock, although it will also be required in the next Mission File.

ANSWERS

TM

1) 07:50
2) Between Stop 3 and Stop 4.

	Time
Stop 1	07:42
Stop 2	07:44
Stop 3	07:46
Stop 4	07:50
Stop 1	07:54
Stop 2	07:56
Stop 3	07:58
Stop 4	08:02
Stop 1	
Stop 2	

3) 08:14 or 8:14 a.m.

MM

1) Huxley knows a mistake has been made because all the times should have an even number of minutes. The shuttle starts at 07:30, which is an even number of minutes. A whole circuit takes 12 minutes and the time between the stops is always an even number.

2)

	Time
Stop 1	09:30
Stop 2	09:32
Stop 3	09:34
Stop 4	09:38
Stop 1	09:42

3) Five times, as there are 5 lots of 12 minutes in one hour.

DV FILES

Stop 1	Stop 1	Stop 1	Stop 2	Stop 3	Stop 4
12:45	13:45	14:45	14:47	14:49	14:53

The shuttle at 15:25 from Stop 3 does not get back to Stop 1 until 15:33 so this is too late. Babs will need to get the shuttle that gets back to Stop 1 at 15:21 so she must catch it at Stop 3 at 15:13.

Stop 1	14:45	14:57	15:09	15:21	15:33
Stop 2	14:47	14:59	15:11	15:23	15:35
Stop 3	14:49	15:01	15:13	15:25	15:37
Stop 4	14:53	15:05	15:17	15:29	15:41
Stop 1	14:57	15:09	15:21	15:33	15:45

MISSION 2.16 Da Vinci's Downtime

MATHEMATICAL CONTENT

- Time (analogue and 24-hour digital)
- Calculating time intervals (minutes and seconds)
- Counting in fraction steps
- Equivalent fractions

TEACHING NOTES

TM Da Vinci's internal clock is running $2\frac{1}{2}$ hours slow. Children must read the time on the analogue clock to calculate first how late Da Vinci is for his 1 o'clock video call and then the time that is showing on the internal clock.

The time shown is to the nearest minute so this makes calculations more challenging when counting back $2\frac{1}{2}$ hours and when finding a time interval. Children may wish to make use of clock resources.

Number lines are useful when working with time intervals.

Children may well do the first two jumps as one larger jump of 46 minutes using bonds to 60.

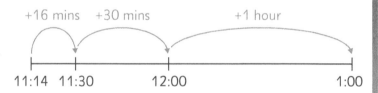

MM A number line is used to present the next problem in the context of a time line.

Children should use what they know about (or find out about) the 24 hour clock to help calculate intervals.

Three of the times are multiples of 5 minutes past each hour, whilst the other is at 29 minutes past.

Look for children who reason about this time being nearly half past, particularly when finding the length of time between the battery recharge at 14:30 and the video call at 19:29, i.e. one minute less than 5 hours.

Questions 3 and 4 require the children to consider Da Vinci's internal clock. Look for those who calculate the end of the meeting as 17:13 and then find the time $2\frac{1}{2}$ hours earlier for Question 4 or those who simply add 1 hour and 6 minutes to their answer for Question 3.

TEACHING NOTES

DV FILES

Disaster strikes as Da Vinci's battery runs out in the middle of an important video call. The children must help the team to charge his back-up battery to reconnect the call in under 3 minutes.

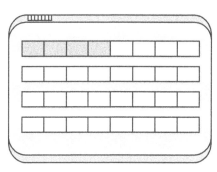

The key information is that it takes 12 seconds to charge $\frac{1}{4}$ of a bar and all bars must be full.

The children should recognise that $\frac{2}{4}$ ($\frac{1}{2}$) of the first bar is already full and then use what they know about the number of quarters in a whole to identify that 12 charges (4 × 3) are needed for 3 bars and an extra 2 for the remainder of the first bar.

Look for children who count less efficiently in quarters ($\frac{2}{8}$) along all bars until 14 is reached.

They should then draw on multiplication facts and partitioning to calculate 12 × 14, e.g. 12 × 10 and then 12 × 4.

Also look for children who reason about the number of charges in a minute, i.e. 12 × 5 = 60 so 5 lots of charges are made in a minute, so there is enough time for 15 charges in 3 minutes and only 14 are needed.

ANSWERS

TM

1) 44 minutes
2) 11:14
3) 1 hour and 46 minutes

MM

1) 4 hours and 59 minutes
2) 3 hours and 6 minutes
3) 13:35
4) 14:43

DV FILES

There are 14 lots of $\frac{1}{4}$ charges to make to fully charge all bars. This means that it will take 12 seconds × 14 = 168 seconds. 3 minutes is 180 seconds so they will make it with 12 seconds to spare!

MISSION 2.17 Playing the Game!

MATHEMATICAL CONTENT

- Money
- Multiplication (including doubling)
- Place value
- Addition and subtraction
- Fractions of amounts

TEACHING NOTES

TM Omar starts with £2000 of his £10,000 inheritance. He begins by buying a number of space hoppers, skipping ropes and table tennis tables. All prices are in pounds with two using decimal pound notation.

Look for children who use doubling and multiplying by 10 to help multiply by 20. Also look for strategies used to multiply by 15, e.g. partitioning as £12.50 × 10 and £12.50 × 5 or finding the price of 10 and then halving to find the price of 5.

Once the total for each toy is found, the children must find the difference between the amount spent and the £2000 to see how much money is left. Look for strategies used as place value of the 50p makes this calculation harder to do in a column (£2000 − £1632.50). A counting on method would work well here, to count up to £1700 (+ 50p + £67) and then add another £300.

MM In the pinball game 500, 250 or 100 points can be scored. Each player has four balls.

The children are given a range of clues that use addition and then fractions of amounts to calculate the score awarded to six different players. Look for children who recognise that 250 + 250 = 500, so quickly calculate Sita's score as 1000.

Children should draw on the effect of adding zero and also on dividing by 10 to find tenths, by 4 to find quarters and by 3 to find thirds. Look for children who may halve and halve again to find a quarter.

Once the total points for each player have been found, the children must also find how the points were scored. Adding zero is key here to help find solutions that would not be possible if all four balls scored points.

TEACHING NOTES

DV FILES

The Da Vinci mission is a logic problem with more than one solution. It is an adaptation of a magic square.

The children are not told the total number of players that should be in each row, but should recognise that

it is likely that one of each game must be in each row and column as there are only three types. A more familiar magic square would use nine different numbers.

Children should find that 12 children in total play one game of each so this will be the sum of all rows and columns if one game of each is placed in them. However, the centre number is key and, therefore, the diagonals are key. With 3 in the centre, one diagonal is 3, 3, 3 (sum of 9 not 12) and with 5 in the centre, one diagonal is 5, 5, 5 (sum of 15 not 12). Only 4 can go in the centre to create the diagonal 4, 4, 4 that does sum to 12. This leads the children to more possibilities as the numbers can be reorganised on the grid. Look for those who recognise that a diagonal must always contain three games of table tennis.

ANSWERS

TM

1) 20 skipping ropes   £2.25 × 20 = £45
   15 space hoppers   £12.50 × 15 = £187.50
   10 table tennis tables £140 × 10 = £1400
   ────────
   £1632.50

2) £2000 − £1632.50 = £367.50

MM

	Total points	Scored by getting
Sita	1000 points	500 + 250 + 250 + 0
Heather	¾ of the points scored by Sita	e.g. 250 + 250 + 250 + 0
Alice	100 more than Heather	e.g. 500 + 250 + 100 + 0
James	4/10 of the points scored by Sita	100 + 100 + 100 + 100
Leo	⅔ of the points scored by Heather	e.g. 250 + 250 + 0 + 0
Finley	Double the points scored by James	500 + 100 + 100 + 100

DV FILES

4	5	3
3	4	5
5	3	4

4	3	5
5	4	3
3	5	4

3	5	4
5	4	3
4	3	5

5	3	4
3	4	5
4	5	3

MISSION 2.18 Beetle Mania!

MATHEMATICAL CONTENT

- Statistics (pictograms)
- Addition and subtraction
- Multiplication and division (including halving)
- Symmetry
- Position and direction
- Multiples of 3, 4, 7 and 9

TEACHING NOTES

TM The pictogram shows the number of the three different species of bug found. As the scale is in twelves, children should use known facts to aid calculation. Look for children who count that there are 10 whole pictures of bugs so this can be found using place value for 12 × 10 and then two halves that require another 12 (or 6 + 6) to be added. This is a much easier strategy than counting in twelves up to 120 and then 132.

In Question 3, children should notice that the scale of the new pictogram is half of the one they have been working with and use this to help make decisions. Look for children who mistakenly halve the number of pictures because 6 is half of 12, instead of realising that it will take two of the new pictures to equal one of the old ones, so twice the number will be required.

MM The children need to use knowledge of symmetry to move the bugs around the grid into a symmetrical pattern. The line of symmetry is in a horizontal position.

The grid uses references familiar in some maps and games like Battleships. Children should record the moves they make as they need to find the least number of moves possible.

In Question 2, the children draw on knowledge of quarter or half turns, right-angle turns and clockwise and anti-clockwise to describe a movement. Look out for children who use degrees in their answers.

TEACHING NOTES

DV FILES

In this mission, the bugs must find a way from the green side of the grid to the red. Each move must be to a hexagon that is joined to the one the bug is currently on.

Each of the three bugs can only move to a hexagon if its value is the product of a calculation that uses at least one of the numbers that belong to each bug.

Children should draw on multiples of 3 and 4 but also derive multiples of 7 and 9 to help find possible solutions. This task is a useful opportunity to assess children's fluency in using multiplication facts.

Encourage the children to look for more than one solution to move each of the bugs. Only Bug J has one solution.

ANSWERS

TM

1) 132 bugs
2) 30 more
3) 7 as 7 × 6 = 42

MM

1)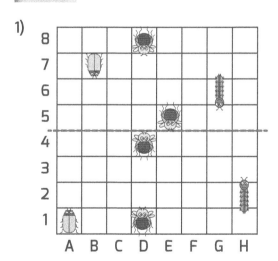

E.g.
Move bug from A1 to B2
Move bug D4 to E4
Move bug from G6 to H7

2) Two right-angle turns (clockwise or anti-clockwise) or two quarter turns or one half turn. It may also be described as a 180° turn or two 90° turns.

DV FILES

3 × 9 = 27
7 × 6 = 42
7 × 20 = 140
3 × 30 = 90
7 × 7 = 49

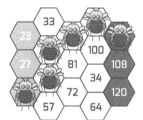

3 × 10 = 30
3 × 16 = 48
7 × 6 or 3 × 14 = 42
7 × 20 = 140
3 × 30 = 90
7 × 7 = 49

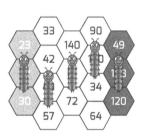

9 × 3 = 27
4 × 12 = 48
9 × 9 = 81
4 × 25 = 100
9 × 12 = 108

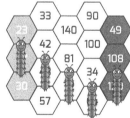

9 × 3 = 27
4 × 12 = 48
9 × 8 = 72
4 × 16 = 64
4 × 30 = 120

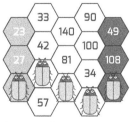

6 × 5 = 30
6 × 8 = 48
8 × 9 = 72 or 6 × 12 = 72
8 × 8 = 64
6 × 20 = 120 or 8 × 15 = 120

MISSION 2.18   45

CURRICULUM MATCHING CHART

Each Brain Academy mission covers a range of mathematical topics and requires children to make connections between areas of mathematics. The chart below shows which areas of the 2014 National Curriculum Programme of Study for Mathematics are covered in each mission.

Domain		Mission 2.1	2.2	2.3	2.4	2.5	2.6
NUMBER	Number	✔					✔
	Place value	✔		✔	✔	✔	
	Estimating						
	Addition and subtraction	✔	✔	✔	✔	✔	✔
	Multiplication and division	✔	✔	✔		✔	✔
	Fractions	✔				✔	
MEASUREMENT	Length			✔	✔		
	Mass/Weight				✔	✔	
	Volume/Capacity						
	Time			✔		✔	
	Money						
GEOMETRY	Properties of shape				✔		
	2-D shapes				✔	✔	
	3-D shapes						
	Position and direction			✔			
STATISTICS					✔		

					Mission						
2.7	2.8	2.9	2.10	2.11	2.12	2.13	2.14	2.15	2.16	2.17	2.18
✔				✔			✔			✔	
							✔				
✔		✔	✔	✔	✔	✔	✔			✔	✔
✔	✔	✔	✔	✔	✔	✔	✔	✔		✔	✔
					✔				✔	✔	
✔	✔		✔	✔	✔	✔					
				✔			✔				
		✔					✔				
	✔		✔	✔				✔	✔		
	✔						✔			✔	
	✔										
		✔									
	✔										
✔			✔	✔							✔
						✔					✔

CURRICULUM MATCHING CHART 47

What is NACE?
NACE, a registered charity founded in 1983, is the leading independent organisation for the education of the more able.

What does NACE do?
NACE specialises in working with teachers and schools to improve learning for the more able and to turn ability into achievement for all.

The NACE community provides teachers with:
A members' website including:
- Guidance and resources
- New to A,G&T
- Subject specific resources
- Specialist advice
- An award winning monthly E-bulletin packed with sources of inspiration and regular updates
- NACE Insight, a termly newsletter

How will the book help me?
The *Brain Academy* Maths Mission Files challenge and help you to become better at learning and a better mathematician by:
- thinking of and testing different solutions to problems
- making connections to what you already know
- working by yourself and with others
- expecting you to get better and to go on to the next book
- learning skills which you can use in other subjects and out of school.

We hope you enjoy the books!